THE ART AND ACTIONS OF CONNECTION

MASTERING COMMUNICATION FOR IMPACT

DR. MINAKSHI BANSAL

To all those who strive to bridge the gaps between us, to listen with open hearts, and to speak with kindness and understanding. May your words and actions create a ripple effect of connection, compassion, and positive change in the world.

Contents

Prayer   *ix*

About The Author   *xi*

Preface   *xv*

1. The Power Of Presence: Active Listening Beyond Words   1

Part 1

2. Empathy Unleashed: Stepping Into Another's Shoes   7

Part 2

3. Decoding Non-Verbal Cues: The Silent Language Of Connection   13

Part 3

4. Words That Build Bridges: Crafting Messages With Clarity And Compassion   19

Part 4

5. Asking Powerful Questions: Igniting Curiosity And Deepening Conversations   25

Part 5

6. Finding Your Authentic Voice: Speaking Your Truth With Confidence   31

Part 6

7. Navigating Conflict With Grace: Transforming Challenges Into Opportunities   37

Part 7

8. The Art Of Storytelling: Weaving Narratives That Captivate And Inspire   43

Part 8

9. Building Rapport: Creating Instant Connections With Anyone   49

Contents

Part 9

10. Feedback As A Gift: Giving And Receiving Constructive   55
Criticism

Part 10

11. Mastering The Art Of Apology: Healing Relationships With   61
Sincerity

Part 11

12. Communication In The Digital Age: Connecting Across   67
Screens

Part 12

13. Leading With Influence: Inspiring Action Through   73
Communication

Part 13

14. Crafting Compelling Presentations: Engaging Your Audience   79
From Start To Finish

Part 14

15. Networking For Success: Building Relationships That Matter   85

Part 15

16. The Power Of Silence: Creating Space For Reflection And   91
Connection

Part 16

17. Humor As A Connector: Bringing Joy And Lightness To   97
Conversations

Part 17

18. Cross-Cultural Communication: Bridging Differences With   103
Understanding

Contents

Part 18

19. The Lifetime Journey Of Communication: Continuous Learning And Growth   109

Part 19

20. Creating A Legacy Of Connection: Making A Positive Impact Through Your Words And Actions   115

Part 20

21. SUMMARY   121

Citation and References   125

Other Books of the Author   127

CONTACT   133

Prayer

"Om Bhadram Karnebhih Shrinuyama Devah

Bhadram Pashyemakshabhiryajatrah

Sthirairangais Tushtuvamsastanubhih

Vyashema Devahitam Yadayuh

Svasti Na Indro Vriddhashravah

Svasti Nah Pusha Vishwavedah

Svasti Nastarkshyo Arishtanemih

Svasti No Brihaspatir Dadhatu

Om Shantih Shantih Shantih"

This mantra is a prayer for universal well-being, invoking the blessings of various deities for protection, health, and happiness. It emphasizes the importance of experiencing the auspicious through all senses and living a life aligned with divine purpose. The repetition of "Shantih" at the end signifies a deep desire for peace in the individual, the environment, and the universe at large. This mantra is often recited as a prayer for peace, prosperity, and the physical and spiritual well-being of all beings.

▷▷▷

About The Author

This book represents the culmination of extensive research and meticulous analysis, incorporating a diverse range of sources, including numerous books, scholarly studies, and personal experiences. Additionally, I have scoured various websites to gather relevant information and data essential for the compilation of this work. I have taken every precaution to ensure the accuracy of the information presented and have diligently cited all sources to acknowledge their contributions.

From her earliest days, Minakshi was distinguished by an insatiable appetite for reading. Her literary universe was inhabited by characters and narratives that spanned ethical tales, motivational and inspirational stories, and the mythic parables imbued with life lessons. This voracious reading habit was not merely for personal edification but was driven by a desire to distill and disseminate the essence of these narratives to foster the development of students and peers alike. She was particularly captivated by the lives and teachings of historical figures and spiritual leaders such as Adi Shankaracharya, Swami Vivekananda, Dr. APJ Abdul Kalam, Mahamana Pandit Madan Mohan Malviya, Mahatma Gandhi, Sardar Vallabhai Patel, and Vinoba Bhave, among others. Their philosophies and life stories fueled her ambition to embody their ideals of resilience, selflessness, and relentless pursuit of knowledge.

Dr. Minakshi's academic and practical engagement with psychology has been equally noteworthy. As a research scholar, her focus has been on exploring the intricate tapestry of the human psyche, aiming to unlock the potential for psychological well-being and societal harmony. Her scholarly work is complemented by her active involvement in social work, where she employs her academic insights to make tangible differences in the lives of the underprivileged. Her endeavours in social work are characterized by an innovative approach that combines traditional wisdom with contemporary psychological practices to address the multifaceted challenges faced by these communities.

Her artistic talents, another facet of her diverse capabilities, are not merely a personal passion but also serve as a medium through which she communicates and connects with others. Her art, rich in symbolism and emotional depth, reflects her philosophical inquiries and social concerns, offering viewers a glimpse into the breadth of her intellect and the depth of her compassion.

In addition to her contributions to the arts and social sciences, Dr. Minakshi has embraced the healing arts of Pranic Healing, mastering the techniques developed by Master Choa Kok Sui. This practice, which focuses on the manipulation of Prana or life energy to heal the body and aura, has been both a personal journey of discovery and a means through which she extends her healing touch to others. Her proficiency in Pranic Healing is complemented by her advocacy and teaching of various forms of meditation aimed at rejuvenation, personal betterment, and the cultivation of harmony within individuals and communities alike.

Dr. Minakshi's life is a narrative of relentless pursuit, not just of personal achievement but of the upliftment and empowerment of society at large. Her diverse interests and talents—spanning the arts, literature, psychology, and the healing practices—converge on a singular path of service. She embodies the spirit of the luminaries who inspired her, channelling their legacy through her actions and teachings. Through her books, art, and social initiatives, she continues to inspire a new generation to embark on their own journeys of self-discovery, resilience, and altruism.

Her commitment to social betterment, particularly her focus on uplifting underprivileged children, reflects a deep understanding of the transformative potential of education and personal development. By integrating her knowledge of psychology, her artistic sensibilities, and her healing practices, Dr. Bansal has developed a holistic approach to social work that addresses both the immediate needs and the long-term well-being of the communities she serves.

As an author, Dr. Minakshi's writings offer a blend of inspirational insights, practical wisdom, and reflective contemplations drawn from her extensive reading and life experiences. Her books serve as a guide for those seeking to navigate the complexities of life with grace, resilience, and purpose. Through her narratives, she extends an invitation to her readers to explore the depths of their own potential and to contribute meaningfully to the collective well-being of society.

In Dr. Minakshi Bansal, we find a remarkable synthesis of the artist, the scholar, the healer, and the social activist. Her life's work stands as a beacon of hope and a source of inspiration for individuals seeking to make a difference in the world. Her story is a compelling reminder of the power of individual action, rooted in compassion and driven by a profound commitment to the betterment of humanity. Dr. Minakshi's legacy is not just in the tangible outcomes of her efforts but in the enduring spirit of inquiry, empathy, and service that she embodies.

ᐅᐅᐅ

Preface

In the tapestry of human existence, connection is the thread that weaves together our experiences, relationships, and understanding of the world. It is the bridge that allows us to share our joys and sorrows, our hopes and fears, our triumphs and failures. It is the foundation upon which we build communities, societies, and a shared sense of purpose.

Communication is the language of connection, the tool through which we express our thoughts, feelings, and ideas. It is the vehicle that carries our stories, our dreams, and our aspirations.

It is the bridge that allows us to cross the chasms of misunderstanding and build bridges of empathy and understanding.

Yet, in a world that is increasingly fragmented and polarized, the art of communication is often overlooked and underappreciated. We are bombarded with information, inundated with distractions, and overwhelmed by the sheer volume of messages vying for our attention. In the midst of this cacophony, we have lost sight of the simple yet profound power of connection.

This book is an invitation to rediscover the art and actions of connection, to master the skills that will allow you to communicate with greater clarity, compassion, and impact. It is a journey of self-discovery, a exploration of the different ways in which we connect with ourselves and others, and a guide to cultivating deeper, more meaningful relationships.

Throughout these pages, you will learn about the importance of presence, the power of empathy, and the art of decoding non-verbal cues. You will discover how to craft messages with clarity and compassion, ask powerful questions, and find your authentic voice.

You will explore the art of storytelling, the nuances of communication in the digital age, and the importance of cross-cultural understanding. You will also learn how to navigate conflict with grace, build rapport with anyone, and give and receive feedback as a gift.

This book is not a magic formula for instant communication success. It is a collection of insights, strategies, and tools that can help you to become a more effective communicator in all areas of your life. It is a journey that requires time, effort, and a willingness to learn and grow. But the rewards are immeasurable.

By mastering the art of communication, you can deepen your relationships, build stronger connections, and make a positive impact on the world. You can become a more effective leader, a more persuasive communicator, and a more compassionate human being.

As you embark on this journey, remember that communication is not just about what you say, but also about how you say it. It's about the tone of your voice, the look in your eyes, and the way you hold yourself. It's about being present, listening deeply, and responding with empathy and understanding.

This book is a testament to the power of connection. It is a reminder that we are all interconnected, that our words and actions have a ripple effect on the world around us.

By choosing to communicate with kindness, compassion, and respect, we can create a more harmonious and fulfilling life for ourselves and others.

As you read these pages, I invite you to embrace the art of

communication with an open heart and a curious mind. May this book inspire you to connect with others in deeper, more meaningful ways, to build stronger relationships, and to make a positive impact on the world.

Dr. Minakshi Bansal
Social Activist
Ahmedabad, Gujarat, Bharat

❦❦❦

ONE

The Power of Presence: Active Listening Beyond Words

In our relentless pursuit of connection, we often overlook the profound power of simply being present. The art of active listening transcends mere words, delving into the realm of genuine understanding and empathy. It's a skill that requires us to tune into the nuances of communication, both spoken and unspoken, to truly hear and connect with the person before us.

At its core, active listening is the act of being fully present with another individual, offering them our undivided attention. It's about setting aside our own thoughts and judgments, silencing the inner monologue, and opening ourselves up to the experience of the other person. When we actively listen, we create a sacred space where the speaker feels heard, validated, and understood.

Active listening goes beyond merely hearing the words being spoken. It involves paying attention to the speaker's non-verbal cues, their tone of voice, facial expressions, and body language. These subtle signals often reveal a wealth of information about the speaker's emotional state and underlying motivations.

By observing these cues, we gain a deeper understanding of the speaker's message and can respond in a more meaningful and compassionate way.

One of the most powerful aspects of active listening is the ability to reflect back what we hear. This doesn't mean simply parroting the speaker's words but rather paraphrasing their message in our own words to ensure that we have understood them correctly.

When we reflect back, we demonstrate that we are actively engaged in the conversation and that we value the speaker's perspective. This simple act can foster a sense of trust and rapport, deepening the connection between us.

Asking open-ended questions is another essential component of active listening. These types of questions encourage the speaker to elaborate on their thoughts and feelings, providing us with a richer understanding of their experience. Open-ended questions often begin with words like "what," "how," or "tell me more about." By asking these questions, we invite the speaker to explore their own thoughts and feelings more deeply, leading to greater self-awareness and insight.

Active listening also involves being mindful of our own internal reactions to what the speaker is saying. We all have biases and preconceived notions that can influence how we interpret and respond to others. By being aware of these biases, we can make a conscious effort to set them aside and listen with an open mind. This allows us to truly hear the speaker's message without filtering it through our own lens of experience.

The benefits of active listening are numerous. When we actively listen to others, we foster a sense of trust and connection. We create a safe space where people feel comfortable sharing their thoughts and feelings openly. This can lead to deeper, more meaningful relationships and greater collaboration. Active listening can also help to resolve conflicts and disagreements.

When we truly understand the other person's perspective, we are better equipped to find common ground and reach mutually agreeable solutions.

In the workplace, active listening is a critical skill for effective leadership. When leaders actively listen to their employees, they create a more engaged and productive workforce. Employees who feel heard and valued are more likely to be motivated and committed to their work. Active listening can also help to identify potential problems and address them before they escalate.

In our personal lives, active listening can strengthen our relationships with family and friends. When we actively listen to our loved ones, we show them that we care about them and value their opinions. This can lead to greater intimacy and connection.

Active listening can also help us to better understand ourselves. By listening to the stories and experiences of others, we can gain new insights and perspectives.

While active listening may seem like a simple concept, it can be challenging to put into practice. We live in a world that is constantly bombarding us with information and distractions. It can be difficult to quiet our minds and focus our attention on the person in front of us. However, with practice, active listening can become a natural and effortless way of interacting with others.

By cultivating the art of active listening, we can transform our relationships, improve our communication skills, and make a positive impact on the world.

When we truly listen to others, we open ourselves up to the possibility of connection, understanding, and growth. We create a space where we can learn from each other, support each other, and celebrate our shared humanity.

ᗑᗑᗑ

Presence is the doorway to understanding. Listen beyond words, tune into emotions, and connect with hearts.

ᐅᐅᐅ

TWO

EMPATHY UNLEASHED: STEPPING INTO ANOTHER'S SHOES

Empathy, often described as "stepping into another's shoes," is the profound ability to understand and share the feelings of another person. It is more than just sympathy, which involves feeling sorry for someone; empathy requires a deeper level of emotional connection and understanding. Unleashing the power of empathy can transform our relationships, both personal and professional, leading to greater understanding, compassion, and connection.

At its core, empathy is about recognizing and validating the emotions of others. It involves putting ourselves in their place and trying to see the world through their eyes. When we empathize with someone, we not only acknowledge their feelings but also try to understand the underlying reasons behind them. This understanding allows us to respond in a way that is both supportive and helpful.

One of the key components of empathy is active listening. When we actively listen to someone, we focus our attention on what they are saying, both verbally and non-verbally. We observe their body language, tone of voice, and facial expressions. We also try to understand the emotions that are driving their words. By actively listening, we create a safe space for the other person to express themselves openly and honestly.

Another important aspect of empathy is perspective-taking. This involves trying to see the situation from the other person's point of view. When we put ourselves in their shoes, we can begin to understand their thoughts, feelings, and motivations. Perspective-taking helps us to avoid making assumptions or judgments about the other person. It also allows us to respond in a way that is more understanding and compassionate.

Empathy also involves emotional regulation. When we empathize with someone, we may experience their emotions as if they were our own. This can be overwhelming, especially if the other person is experiencing intense emotions like sadness, anger, or fear. Emotional regulation allows us to manage our own emotions while still being present for the other person. It involves recognizing and acknowledging our own feelings while also maintaining a sense of calm and composure.

The benefits of empathy are numerous. When we practice empathy, we strengthen our relationships with others. We build trust, understanding, and connection. We also become better communicators, as we are more able to listen to and understand the perspectives of others. Empathy can also help to reduce conflict and promote cooperation. When we see things from another person's point of view, we are less likely to become defensive or reactive. We are also more likely to find common ground and work together towards solutions.

In the workplace, empathy is a valuable skill for leaders and managers. When leaders empathize with their employees, they create a more positive and supportive work environment. Employees who feel understood and valued are more likely to be engaged and productive. They are also more likely to trust their leaders and be willing to go the extra mile.

In our personal lives, empathy can help us to build stronger relationships with our family and friends. When we empathize with our loved ones, we show them that we care about them and value their feelings. This can lead to deeper, more meaningful relationships. Empathy can also help us to navigate difficult conversations and resolve conflicts.

While empathy is a natural human capacity, it is a skill that can be developed and strengthened through practice. There are many things we can do to cultivate empathy. One simple way is to actively listen to others. When someone is speaking to you, give them your full attention. Put away your phone, turn off the TV, and make eye contact. Listen not only to their words but also to their tone of voice, body language, and facial expressions.

Another way to cultivate empathy is to practice perspective-taking. When you are faced with a situation, try to see it from the other person's point of view. Ask yourself how they might be feeling and what their motivations might be. This can help you to understand their behavior and respond in a more compassionate way.

You can also practice empathy by reading books, watching movies, or listening to music that explores the experiences of others. This can help you to develop a deeper understanding of different perspectives and cultures.

By unleashing the power of empathy, we can create a more compassionate and connected world. When we understand and share the feelings of others, we build stronger relationships, reduce conflict, and promote cooperation. Empathy is a powerful tool that can transform our lives and the lives of those around us.

❧❧❧

Empathy is the bridge between souls. Walk in another's shoes, feel their joys and sorrows, and build bridges of compassion.

❥❥❥

THREE

Decoding Non-Verbal Cues: The Silent Language of Connection

In the intricate dance of human communication, words are but one part of the story. A vast realm of unspoken signals, gestures, and expressions exists beneath the surface, forming a silent language that often speaks louder than words. Decoding these non-verbal cues is essential for truly understanding and connecting with others on a deeper level.

Non-verbal communication encompasses a wide range of behaviors, including facial expressions, body language, posture, eye contact, touch, and even the use of space. These cues often reveal our true emotions, intentions, and attitudes, even when our words might suggest otherwise. By learning to read and interpret these signals, we can gain valuable insights into the thoughts and feelings of others, enhancing our ability to communicate effectively and build stronger relationships.

Facial expressions are perhaps the most universal and easily recognizable form of non-verbal communication. A smile, a frown, a raised eyebrow, or a furrowed brow can convey a wealth of information about a person's emotional state. Our faces are incredibly expressive, capable of conveying a wide range of emotions, from joy and excitement to sadness, anger, and fear. By paying attention to these subtle shifts in expression, we can gain a deeper understanding of how someone is feeling and respond accordingly.

Body language is another powerful form of non-verbal communication. The way we hold ourselves, the gestures we use, and the movements we make can all reveal our thoughts and feelings. Crossed arms might suggest defensiveness or resistance, while open arms might indicate openness and receptivity. Leaning forward can signal interest and engagement, while leaning back might suggest disinterest or boredom. By observing these subtle cues, we can gain valuable insights into the attitudes and intentions of others.

Eye contact is a particularly important form of non-verbal communication. The eyes are often referred to as the "windows to the soul," and for good reason. Maintaining eye contact conveys interest, attention, and confidence. Avoiding eye contact, on the other hand, can signal discomfort, disinterest, or even deceit. The duration and intensity of eye contact can also vary depending on the cultural context and the relationship between the individuals involved.

Touch is another form of non-verbal communication that can convey a wide range of emotions, from affection and comfort to dominance and aggression. A gentle touch on the arm can express empathy and support, while a firm handshake can convey confidence and authority. However, it's important to be mindful of cultural and personal boundaries when it comes to touch, as what might be appropriate in one context might not be in another.

The use of space, or proxemics, is another aspect of non-verbal communication that can reveal a lot about our relationships with others. The distance we maintain between ourselves and others can indicate our level of intimacy, comfort, and familiarity. Standing close to someone might suggest closeness and trust, while maintaining a greater distance might indicate formality or respect.

The tone of voice, or paralanguage, is another important element of non-verbal communication. The way we speak, including our pitch, volume, and intonation, can convey a wide range of emotions and attitudes. A soft, gentle voice might suggest warmth and compassion, while a loud, harsh voice might indicate anger or frustration.

Decoding non-verbal cues is not always easy, as the meaning of these signals can vary depending on the context, the individual, and the culture. However, by paying attention to these subtle signals and learning to interpret them in context, we can gain a deeper understanding of the people around us and communicate more effectively.

It's important to remember that non-verbal communication is often unconscious and automatic. We may not even be aware of the signals we are sending out. However, by becoming more mindful of our own non-verbal cues, we can learn to communicate more intentionally and authentically.

Ultimately, the ability to decode non-verbal cues is a valuable skill that can enhance our relationships, improve our communication, and deepen our understanding of ourselves and others. By learning to read the silent language of connection, we can unlock a whole new world of communication and build stronger, more meaningful relationships.

❦❦❦

Words are seeds that can bloom into gardens of connection. Choose them wisely, nurture them with kindness, and watch them grow.

ᗑᗑᗑ

FOUR

WORDS THAT BUILD BRIDGES: CRAFTING MESSAGES WITH CLARITY AND COMPASSION

Words possess an extraordinary power. They can uplift, inspire, and heal, or they can wound, divide, and destroy. Crafting messages with clarity and compassion is an art that enables us to build bridges of understanding, forge deeper connections, and foster positive change in the world.

At the heart of effective communication lies clarity. When our messages are clear, concise, and easy to understand, they are more likely to resonate with our audience and achieve their intended purpose. Clarity begins with a clear understanding of our own thoughts and feelings. Before we can communicate effectively with others, we must first be clear about what we want to say and why it matters.

Once we have clarity about our message, we can begin to craft it in a way that is both compelling and easy to understand. This involves using simple, direct language, avoiding jargon and technical terms, and organizing our thoughts in a logical and coherent way. It also means being mindful of our tone of voice and non-verbal cues, which can significantly impact how our message is received.

While clarity is essential, it is not enough on its own. Compassion is the key that unlocks the true potential of our words. When we communicate with compassion, we acknowledge and validate the feelings of others. We show that we care about their well-being and that we are committed to building a positive relationship with them.

Compassionate communication involves listening attentively to others, seeking to understand their perspective, and responding with empathy and kindness. It means choosing our words carefully, avoiding judgment and criticism, and focusing on solutions rather than blame. When we communicate with compassion, we create a safe space for open dialogue and collaboration, where everyone feels heard and valued.

Crafting messages with clarity and compassion is not always easy. It requires us to be mindful of our own biases and assumptions, to be willing to listen to different perspectives, and to be open to feedback. It also requires us to be patient and persistent, as building trust and understanding takes time and effort.

However, the rewards of compassionate communication are immeasurable. When we communicate with clarity and compassion, we create a ripple effect of positivity that can extend far beyond our immediate interactions. We build stronger relationships, foster greater understanding, and create a more harmonious and inclusive world.

In the workplace, compassionate communication is essential for building a positive and productive work environment. When leaders communicate with clarity and compassion, they create a culture of trust and respect, where employees feel valued and empowered. This leads to increased engagement, productivity, and innovation.

In our personal lives, compassionate communication can strengthen our relationships with family and friends. When we communicate with our loved ones in a way that is both clear and compassionate, we create a deeper sense of connection and intimacy. We also build trust and understanding, which are essential for healthy relationships.

Compassionate communication is not just about the words we use; it's about the intention behind them. When we communicate with the intention of connecting with others, of understanding their perspective, and of fostering positive change, our words take on a new power. They become tools for building bridges, healing wounds, and creating a better world.

In a world that is often divided by conflict and misunderstanding, the power of words to build bridges cannot be overstated. By crafting messages with clarity and compassion, we can break down barriers, heal divisions, and create a more harmonious and interconnected world.

ᐁᐁᐁ

Questions are the keys that unlock the chambers of the mind. Ask with curiosity, explore with wonder, and discover hidden treasures.

❥❥❥

FIVE

ASKING POWERFUL QUESTIONS: IGNITING CURIOSITY AND DEEPENING CONVERSATIONS

Questions are the spark plugs of conversations. They ignite curiosity, deepen understanding, and propel dialogue forward. But not all questions are created equal. Powerful questions possess a unique ability to unlock new insights, challenge assumptions, and inspire meaningful connections.

At their core, powerful questions are open-ended inquiries that invite exploration and discovery. Unlike closed-ended questions, which elicit simple yes or no answers, powerful questions encourage thoughtful reflection and expansive responses. They delve beneath the surface, probing into the underlying thoughts, feelings, and motivations of the person being questioned.

One of the hallmarks of a powerful question is its ability to challenge assumptions. By inviting the listener to consider alternative perspectives and possibilities, powerful questions can break down mental barriers and open up new avenues for thought. They can spark aha moments, where previously hidden truths are revealed and new connections are made.

Powerful questions also have the power to ignite curiosity. By piquing our interest and sparking our imagination, they can lead us down unexpected paths of discovery. They can encourage us to question the status quo, to explore uncharted territories, and to seek out new knowledge and experiences.

In conversations, powerful questions can serve as a catalyst for deeper connection. By asking thoughtful and probing questions, we can show genuine interest in the other person and their perspective. We can create a safe space for them to share their thoughts and feelings openly and honestly. This can lead to greater understanding, empathy, and trust.

Powerful questions can also be used to facilitate problem-solving and decision-making. By asking questions that explore the root causes of a problem, we can gain a deeper understanding of the issue at hand. By asking questions that consider different options and potential outcomes, we can make more informed and effective decisions.

In the workplace, powerful questions can be a valuable tool for leaders and managers. By asking questions that challenge assumptions and encourage critical thinking, leaders can foster a culture of innovation and continuous improvement. By asking questions that promote collaboration and teamwork, leaders can create a more engaged and productive workforce.

In our personal lives, powerful questions can help us to deepen our relationships with friends and family. By asking questions that show genuine interest in their lives and perspectives, we can strengthen our bonds and create lasting memories. By asking questions that explore our own thoughts and feelings, we can gain greater self-awareness and insight.

So, what makes a question powerful? There are several key characteristics:

Open-endedness: Powerful questions are open-ended, meaning they cannot be answered with a simple yes or no. They invite the listener to share their thoughts, feelings, and experiences in their own words.

Curiosity: Powerful questions are fueled by genuine curiosity. They are asked with the intention of learning and understanding, not judging or criticizing.

Challenge: Powerful questions challenge assumptions and invite the listener to consider alternative perspectives. They can be provocative, thought-provoking, and even a little uncomfortable.

Focus: Powerful questions are focused and specific. They are not vague or overly broad. They are designed to elicit a particular type of response or information.

Empowerment: Powerful questions empower the listener to think for themselves and come to their own conclusions. They do not impose a particular viewpoint or agenda.

Examples of powerful questions include:

What are you most passionate about?

What is your biggest challenge right now?
What are you most grateful for?
What is your vision for the future?
What would you do if you knew you could not fail?
What is one thing you can do today to move closer to your goals?
What is the most important thing you have learned in your life?

By asking powerful questions, we can ignite curiosity, deepen conversations, and create meaningful connections. We can challenge assumptions, spark new ideas, and inspire positive change. Powerful questions are a tool for personal growth, professional development, and social impact. They are a gift we can give to ourselves and others, a way of opening up new possibilities and creating a better world.

ᐅᐅᐅ

Your voice is a melody waiting to be sung. Embrace your authenticity, speak your truth with courage, and let your melody resonate.

ᗬᗬᗬ

SIX

FINDING YOUR AUTHENTIC VOICE: SPEAKING YOUR TRUTH WITH CONFIDENCE

In a world that often encourages conformity and masks, finding and expressing your authentic voice can be a transformative journey. It is the process of unearthing your true self, embracing your unique perspective, and communicating your thoughts and feelings with honesty and conviction. Speaking your truth with confidence is not merely about being loud or assertive; it's about aligning your words with your values, beliefs, and experiences.

Authenticity begins with self-discovery. It requires delving into the depths of your being to understand your passions, desires, fears, and dreams. It involves recognizing and accepting your strengths and weaknesses, your quirks and idiosyncrasies. It's about embracing your whole self, not just the parts that you think others will approve of.

As you embark on this journey of self-discovery, you may encounter internal resistance. Fear of judgment, rejection, or vulnerability can hold you back from fully expressing yourself. However, it is important to remember that your voice matters. Your unique perspective has value and deserves to be heard. By silencing your authentic voice, you not only deny yourself the opportunity to connect with others on a deeper level but also deprive the world of your unique gifts and talents.

Finding your authentic voice is not a one-time event but an ongoing process. It requires continuous self-reflection, exploration, and growth. It involves challenging your assumptions, questioning your beliefs, and expanding your horizons. It's about being open to new experiences, learning from your mistakes, and evolving as a person.

One of the keys to finding your authentic voice is to cultivate self-awareness. This means paying attention to your thoughts, feelings, and bodily sensations. It involves recognizing the triggers that cause you to react in certain ways and understanding the underlying beliefs that shape your worldview. By becoming more self-aware, you can identify the patterns and habits that hold you back from expressing your true self.

Another important aspect of finding your authentic voice is to develop self-acceptance. This means embracing all aspects of yourself, both the light and the shadow. It involves recognizing that your imperfections are what make you unique and that your vulnerabilities are what make you human. By accepting yourself fully, you create a foundation of self-love and confidence that allows you to speak your truth without fear of judgment or rejection.

Once you have found your authentic voice, the next step is to express it with confidence. This doesn't mean being arrogant or overbearing, but rather speaking your truth in a way that is clear, direct, and respectful. It means being willing to stand up for what you believe in, even when it's unpopular or controversial.

Speaking your truth with confidence requires courage and vulnerability. It means being willing to put yourself out there, to risk rejection and criticism. However, the rewards of speaking your truth far outweigh the risks. When you speak your truth with confidence, you not only inspire others to do the same but also create a ripple effect of positive change in the world.

In the workplace, finding and expressing your authentic voice can lead to greater career satisfaction and success. When you align your work with your values and passions, you are more likely to feel fulfilled and motivated. You are also more likely to be seen as a leader and an innovator, as your unique perspective can bring fresh ideas and solutions to the table.

In your personal relationships, speaking your truth with confidence can deepen your connections with others. When you are open and honest about your thoughts and feelings, you create a space for deeper intimacy and understanding. You also set healthy boundaries and ensure that your needs are met.

Finding your authentic voice is a journey of self-discovery, self-acceptance, and self-expression. It is a journey that requires courage, vulnerability, and a willingness to embrace your unique perspective. But the rewards are immeasurable. When you speak your truth with confidence, you not only empower yourself but also inspire others to do the same.

ᗢᗢᗢ

Conflict is not a battle to be won, but an opportunity for growth. Navigate with grace, seek understanding, and emerge stronger together.

ᗡᗡᗡ

SEVEN

Navigating Conflict with Grace: Transforming Challenges into Opportunities

Conflict is an inevitable part of human interaction. Whether it's a disagreement with a loved one, a clash of opinions at work, or a misunderstanding between friends, conflict can arise in any relationship. However, conflict doesn't have to be destructive. In fact, when navigated with grace, conflict can be transformed into an opportunity for growth, understanding, and stronger connections.

Navigating conflict with grace begins with a shift in perspective. Instead of viewing conflict as a battle to be won or lost, we can approach it as a chance to learn and grow. This means recognizing that conflict is not a sign of failure but rather an opportunity to deepen our understanding of ourselves and others.

One of the key elements of navigating conflict with grace is effective communication. This involves listening actively to the other person's perspective, expressing our own thoughts and feelings clearly and respectfully, and seeking to understand the underlying needs and interests of both parties. It also means being willing to compromise and find solutions that work for everyone involved.

When emotions run high, it can be difficult to communicate effectively. However, it's important to remember that conflict is not about winning or losing. It's about finding a way to move forward together. By focusing on the issue at hand, rather than on personal attacks or accusations, we can create a more productive and respectful dialogue.

Another important aspect of navigating conflict with grace is empathy. This means putting ourselves in the other person's shoes and trying to understand their perspective, even if we don't agree with it. When we empathize with others, we are more likely to find common ground and reach a mutually agreeable solution.

Forgiveness is also a crucial component of navigating conflict with grace. Holding onto anger and resentment only prolongs the conflict and damages relationships. By forgiving others, we free ourselves from the burden of negativity and open the door to reconciliation and healing.

It's important to remember that navigating conflict with grace doesn't mean being a pushover or avoiding difficult conversations. It means standing up for ourselves and our values while also respecting the other person's perspective. It means being willing to engage in difficult conversations with an open mind and a compassionate heart.

In the workplace, navigating conflict with grace can lead to greater productivity, collaboration, and innovation. When employees feel safe to express their opinions and concerns, they are more likely to be engaged and invested in their work. By fostering a culture of respect and open communication, organizations can create a more positive and productive work environment.

In our personal lives, navigating conflict with grace can strengthen our relationships with family and friends. When we are able to resolve conflicts in a healthy and constructive way, we build trust, intimacy, and connection. We also learn to appreciate our differences and grow together as individuals.

Navigating conflict with grace is not always easy. It requires patience, understanding, and a willingness to let go of ego and control. However, the rewards are immeasurable. When we approach conflict with grace, we create a ripple effect of positivity that can extend far beyond the immediate situation. We build stronger relationships, foster greater understanding, and create a more peaceful and harmonious world.

In the words of Mahatma Gandhi, "An eye for an eye makes the whole world blind." By choosing to navigate conflict with grace, we can break the cycle of violence and create a more compassionate and connected world.

ppp

Rapport is the spark that ignites connection. Find common ground, share laughter, and watch the sparks fly.

ﬗﬗﬗ

EIGHT

THE ART OF STORYTELLING: WEAVING NARRATIVES THAT CAPTIVATE AND INSPIRE

Storytelling is a timeless art that has captivated and inspired humanity since the dawn of time. It's a universal language that transcends cultures, languages, and generations. Stories have the power to transport us to different worlds, evoke deep emotions, and challenge our perspectives. They can entertain, educate, and inspire us to action. But what is it about stories that makes them so powerful? And how can we harness this power to create narratives that truly captivate and inspire?

At its core, storytelling is about creating a shared experience. When we tell a story, we invite our listeners to enter a world of our creation, to see through the eyes of our characters, and to feel their joys and sorrows. Stories have the power to connect us to one another on a deep, emotional level. They allow us to tap into our shared humanity and to find meaning and purpose in our lives.

But storytelling is not just about entertaining or connecting with others. Stories can also be a powerful tool for education and persuasion. They can help us to understand complex concepts, remember important information, and make sense of the world around us. Stories can also inspire us to action, to challenge the status quo, and to make a difference in the world.

So, what makes a story captivating and inspiring? There are many elements that contribute to the power of a story, but some of the most important include:

Characters: The characters in a story are the heart and soul of the narrative. They are the ones we root for, empathize with, and learn from. Compelling characters are complex, relatable, and believable. They have strengths and weaknesses, flaws and virtues. They make mistakes, learn from them, and grow as individuals.

Conflict: Conflict is the engine that drives a story forward. It creates tension, suspense, and drama. Conflict can be internal, such as a character struggling with their own demons, or external, such as a battle between good and evil. Without conflict, a story can feel flat and uninteresting.

Theme: The theme of a story is its underlying message or meaning. It is the universal truth that the story explores. Themes can be about love, loss, betrayal, redemption, courage, hope, or any number of other topics. A strong theme can give a story depth and resonance, making it stay with us long after we've finished reading or listening to it.

Structure: The structure of a story is the way in which the events are organized. A well-structured story has a clear beginning, middle, and end. It builds suspense and anticipation, leading to a satisfying climax and resolution.

Language: The language of a story is the way in which the author uses words to create images, evoke emotions, and convey meaning. Vivid and evocative language can bring a story to life, making it more engaging and memorable.

While there is no single formula for creating a captivating and inspiring story, there are certain techniques that can help you to craft a narrative that will resonate with your audience. These techniques include:

Show, don't tell: Instead of simply telling your audience what is happening, show them through vivid descriptions, dialogue, and action. This will help to create a more immersive and engaging experience for your listeners.

Use sensory details: Engage your audience's senses by describing sights, sounds, smells, tastes, and textures. This will help to create a more vivid and believable world for them to inhabit.

Create a sense of suspense and anticipation: Keep your audience guessing by introducing conflict, twists, and turns. This will help to keep them engaged and invested in the story.

Build emotional connection: Tap into your audience's emotions by creating characters they can relate to and situations that resonate with their own experiences. This will help to make your story more meaningful and memorable.

End with a bang: Leave your audience with a lasting impression by crafting a satisfying conclusion that resolves the conflict and leaves them with something to think about.

The art of storytelling is a powerful tool that can be used to entertain, educate, persuade, and inspire. By understanding the elements that make a story captivating and by using effective storytelling techniques, you can create narratives that will leave a lasting impact on your audience. Whether you are a writer, a speaker, or simply someone who wants to share their story with the world, the art of storytelling is a skill that is worth mastering.

ᐅᐅᐅ

Feedback is a gift, wrapped in honesty and tied with care. Give it with kindness, receive it with grace, and unwrap the potential within.

ᗁᗁᗁ

NINE

BUILDING RAPPORT: CREATING INSTANT CONNECTIONS WITH ANYONE

The ability to build rapport – that feeling of connection, understanding, and trust – is a skill that can transform interactions from mundane to meaningful. It's the invisible thread that weaves together relationships, whether personal or professional, and allows for smoother communication, collaboration, and mutual respect.

While some may believe rapport is a matter of inherent charm or luck, it's actually a skill that can be cultivated and honed with practice.

At its core, building rapport is about establishing common ground and creating a sense of shared understanding. It's about finding those points of connection that make us feel seen, heard, and valued by the person we're interacting with.

While it may seem like a daunting task to create instant connections with anyone, there are several key strategies that can be employed to foster rapport quickly and effectively.

One of the most fundamental aspects of building rapport is active listening. When we truly listen to someone, we pay attention not just to their words but also to their tone of voice, body language, and facial expressions. We ask clarifying questions, summarize what we've heard, and express empathy and understanding. This demonstrates that we value their perspective and are genuinely interested in what they have to say.

Another crucial element of building rapport is mirroring. This involves subtly mimicking the other person's body language, tone of voice, and even speech patterns. When done subtly, mirroring can create a sense of unconscious rapport and make the other person feel more comfortable and at ease.

Finding common ground is another key strategy for building rapport. This could involve discovering shared interests, experiences, or values. Even small things, like a mutual appreciation for a certain type of music or a shared experience of growing up in a particular area, can create a sense of connection and camaraderie.

Asking open-ended questions is also a powerful tool for building rapport. Unlike closed-ended questions, which can be answered with a simple yes or no, open-ended questions invite the other person to share their thoughts, feelings, and experiences. This can lead to deeper conversations, greater understanding, and stronger connections.

Sharing personal stories and experiences can also be an effective way to build rapport. When we open up and share something about ourselves, we create an opportunity for the other person to reciprocate. This can lead to a sense of mutual vulnerability and trust, which are essential ingredients for building rapport.

Humor can also be a powerful tool for building rapport. A well-timed joke or a playful remark can break the ice, lighten the mood, and create a sense of shared enjoyment. However, it's important to be mindful of the context and the other person's sense of humor to avoid inadvertently offending or alienating them.

In addition to these verbal and non-verbal communication strategies, there are also several mindset shifts that can help us build rapport more effectively. One of these is to approach interactions with a genuine curiosity and interest in the other person.

When we are truly curious about someone, we are more likely to ask engaging questions, listen attentively, and find common ground.

Another important mindset shift is to focus on the present moment. When we are fully present with the person we're interacting with, we are more likely to notice their non-verbal cues, respond authentically, and create a genuine connection.

It's also important to be mindful of our own energy and emotions. When we are feeling stressed, anxious, or distracted, it can be difficult to build rapport with others. Taking a few deep breaths, centering ourselves, and focusing on the present moment can help us to be more present and engaged in our interactions.

Building rapport is a skill that takes practice and effort, but the rewards are well worth it. When we are able to create instant connections with others, we open up a world of possibilities for collaboration, communication, and mutual respect.

Whether we are networking for a new job, building relationships with clients, or simply making new friends, the ability to build rapport is an invaluable asset that can enrich our lives in countless ways.

In the end, building rapport is about more than just making a good impression or getting what we want. It's about creating meaningful connections with others, fostering understanding and empathy, and building a more compassionate and connected world. By cultivating the art of rapport, we can unlock the power of human connection and create a more positive and fulfilling life for ourselves and those around us.

ppp

Apology is a balm for wounded hearts. Acknowledge the pain, express remorse, and offer a sincere apology to mend broken bridges.

♥♥♥

TEN

FEEDBACK AS A GIFT: GIVING AND RECEIVING CONSTRUCTIVE CRITICISM

In the intricate dance of personal and professional growth, feedback emerges as a powerful catalyst. Often perceived as a daunting experience, both giving and receiving feedback, particularly constructive criticism, can be a transformative process when approached with the right mindset. By viewing feedback as a gift, we unlock its potential to fuel improvement, strengthen relationships, and cultivate a culture of continuous learning.

At its core, feedback is information provided about a person's performance or behavior. It can be positive, highlighting strengths and accomplishments, or constructive, pointing out areas for improvement.

While positive feedback is often welcomed with open arms, constructive criticism can be more challenging to receive. However, it is precisely this type of feedback that holds the greatest potential for growth.

Constructive criticism, when delivered thoughtfully and received openly, can illuminate blind spots, challenge assumptions, and spark new ideas. It can help us identify areas where we can improve, develop new skills, and achieve our goals more effectively. In essence, constructive criticism is a gift that can help us become the best version of ourselves.

Giving constructive criticism requires a delicate balance of honesty and tact. It's important to be specific and focus on the behavior or action rather than the person. Instead of saying, "You're always late," a more constructive approach would be to say, "I noticed that you were late for the meeting this morning.

Is there anything I can do to help you be on time in the future?" By focusing on the behavior, we avoid personal attacks and create a more open and collaborative environment.

It's also important to frame constructive criticism in a way that is both encouraging and motivating. Instead of focusing on the negative, highlight the potential for growth and improvement. For example, instead of saying, "Your presentation was disorganized," you could say, "Your presentation had some great ideas, but it could be more impactful with a clearer structure and more visuals."

By offering specific suggestions for improvement, you empower the recipient to take action and make positive changes.

Receiving constructive criticism can be equally challenging. It's natural to feel defensive or hurt when our work or behavior is criticized. However, it's important to remember that feedback is not a personal attack but rather an opportunity for growth. By approaching feedback with an open mind and a willingness to learn, we can extract valuable insights that can help us improve and succeed.

One of the most effective ways to receive constructive criticism is to listen actively and without judgment. This means paying attention to what the person is saying, asking clarifying questions if needed, and summarizing what you've heard to ensure understanding.

It also means avoiding interrupting or becoming defensive. By actively listening, we demonstrate respect for the feedback giver and create a space for open dialogue.

It's also helpful to ask for specific examples of the behavior or action being criticized. This can help us understand the feedback more clearly and identify concrete steps we can take to improve. For example, if someone says, "You need to be more assertive," you could ask, "Can you give me an example of a situation where I could have been more assertive?"

Once you have received feedback, take some time to reflect on it. Consider whether the feedback is accurate and relevant. If so, identify specific actions you can take to improve. If not, don't be afraid to respectfully disagree or ask for clarification. The goal is to learn from the feedback, not to simply accept it blindly.

By viewing feedback as a gift, we can transform it from a potentially negative experience into a positive one. We can learn from our mistakes, grow as individuals, and build stronger relationships.

When we approach feedback with an open mind and a willingness to learn, we create a culture of continuous improvement where everyone feels valued and supported.

Remember, feedback is not about tearing people down; it's about building them up. When we give and receive feedback with clarity, compassion, and a focus on growth, we create a powerful tool for personal and professional development.

By embracing feedback as a gift, we unlock its potential to transform our lives and the lives of those around us.

ᐳᐳᐳ

*In the digital age, connection is more important
than ever. Reach across screens, bridge the distance,
and nurture virtual bonds with care.*

ᐅᐅᐅ

ELEVEN

MASTERING THE ART OF APOLOGY: HEALING RELATIONSHIPS WITH SINCERITY

The art of apology is a delicate dance of humility, empathy, and accountability. It's a powerful tool that can mend broken trust, heal wounds, and restore harmony to relationships. However, not all apologies are created equal. A sincere apology goes beyond mere words; it requires a genuine acknowledgment of wrongdoing, a willingness to take responsibility for our actions, and a commitment to making amends.

At its core, an apology is an expression of regret for the harm we have caused another person. It's a recognition that our actions or words have hurt someone, whether intentionally or unintentionally. A sincere apology conveys remorse, empathy, and a desire to repair the damage we have caused.

The first step in mastering the art of apology is to acknowledge the harm we have caused. This means recognizing the impact of our actions on the other person and taking responsibility for our role in the situation. It's not about making excuses or justifying our behavior but rather about owning up to our mistakes and acknowledging the pain we have caused.

Once we have acknowledged the harm, the next step is to express remorse. This means conveying our genuine regret for the hurt we have caused. It's not enough to simply say "I'm sorry"; we must also express empathy for the other person's feelings and show that we understand the impact of our actions.

The third step in a sincere apology is to offer a genuine apology. This means taking responsibility for our actions and expressing a willingness to make amends. It's not about offering a halfhearted "sorry" or trying to minimize the harm we have caused. It's about expressing a sincere desire to repair the damage and rebuild trust.

In addition to these three essential elements, a sincere apology may also involve taking concrete steps to make amends. This could include offering a tangible gesture of remorse, such as a gift or a handwritten note. It could also involve taking steps to change our behavior in the future, such as attending therapy or making a commitment to communicate more effectively.

It's important to note that a sincere apology is not about groveling or self-flagellation. It's about recognizing the harm we have caused and taking responsibility for it. It's about expressing remorse and empathy, and offering a genuine apology. It's about demonstrating a commitment to making amends and rebuilding trust.

When done sincerely, an apology can be a powerful tool for healing relationships. It can help to mend broken trust, reduce anger and resentment, and foster forgiveness. It can also pave the way for deeper understanding, stronger connections, and a more positive future together.

However, it's important to remember that an apology is not a magic wand. It doesn't erase the harm that has been done, nor does it guarantee forgiveness. It is simply a first step towards healing and reconciliation.

The recipient of an apology also plays a crucial role in the healing process. They have the right to accept or reject the apology, to forgive or not to forgive. Forgiveness is a personal choice that cannot be forced or demanded. However, when both parties are willing to engage in open and honest communication, forgiveness becomes possible.

In the end, the art of apology is about more than just saying "I'm sorry." It's about recognizing the harm we have caused, taking responsibility for our actions, and expressing remorse and empathy. It's about offering a genuine apology and taking concrete steps to make amends. It's about acknowledging the pain we have caused and seeking to rebuild trust. It's about opening our hearts to forgiveness and creating a space for healing and reconciliation.

ɔɔɔ

*Leadership is not about power, but about influence.
Inspire action through your words, motivate with
your vision, and lead with empathy.*

❥❥❥

TWELVE

COMMUNICATION IN THE DIGITAL AGE: CONNECTING ACROSS SCREENS

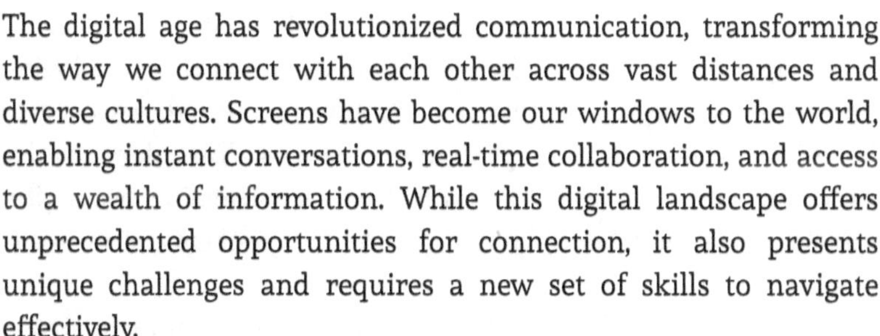

The digital age has revolutionized communication, transforming the way we connect with each other across vast distances and diverse cultures. Screens have become our windows to the world, enabling instant conversations, real-time collaboration, and access to a wealth of information. While this digital landscape offers unprecedented opportunities for connection, it also presents unique challenges and requires a new set of skills to navigate effectively.

In the digital realm, communication transcends geographical boundaries, connecting individuals from different corners of the globe. Social media platforms, messaging apps, and video conferencing tools have made it easier than ever to stay in touch with loved ones, build professional networks, and participate in global communities. We can now exchange ideas, share experiences, and collaborate on projects with people from all walks of life, fostering a sense of interconnectedness and cultural exchange.

However, digital communication also presents challenges that can hinder genuine connection. The absence of non-verbal cues, such as facial expressions and body language, can make it difficult to interpret tone and intent, leading to misunderstandings and miscommunications. The sheer volume of information and constant notifications can be overwhelming, leading to information overload and a sense of disconnect.

To navigate the digital landscape effectively, we need to develop new communication skills and strategies. One of the most important is to be mindful of our digital footprint. Every message we send, every post we share, and every comment we leave contributes to our online identity. It's important to be thoughtful and intentional about our digital communication, ensuring that it aligns with our values and goals.

Another key skill is to be adaptable and flexible. The digital landscape is constantly evolving, with new platforms, technologies, and trends emerging all the time. To stay connected, we need to be willing to learn and adapt to these changes. This might involve experimenting with new communication tools, learning new digital etiquette, or simply being open to different ways of communicating.

In the digital age, effective communication also requires a strong sense of empathy and emotional intelligence. While we may not be able to see the person we're communicating with, it's important to remember that there is a real person on the other side of the screen. By putting ourselves in their shoes and considering their perspective, we can communicate with greater understanding and compassion.

One of the challenges of digital communication is the potential for misinterpretation. Sarcasm, humor, and irony can be difficult to convey through text alone. To avoid misunderstandings, it's important to be clear and concise in our communication. Using emojis or emoticons can help to convey tone and emotion, but it's always best to err on the side of clarity.

Building trust is also essential for effective digital communication. In the absence of face-to-face interaction, it can be more difficult to establish trust with someone we've only met online. To build trust, it's important to be transparent, honest, and authentic in our communication. We should also be mindful of our privacy settings and be careful about what information we share online.

While digital communication offers many benefits, it's important to maintain a healthy balance between online and offline interactions. Spending too much time in front of screens can lead to social isolation, decreased physical activity, and a host of other health problems. It's important to make time for face-to-face interactions with loved ones, friends, and colleagues.

In the workplace, digital communication tools have transformed the way we collaborate and work together. Virtual meetings, shared documents, and project management software have made it possible for teams to work together seamlessly, regardless of their location. However, it's important to establish clear communication guidelines and expectations to ensure that everyone is on the same page.

In education, digital communication tools have opened up new possibilities for learning and collaboration. Online courses, virtual classrooms, and discussion forums have made education more accessible and flexible. However, it's important for educators to be mindful of the challenges of digital communication and to provide students with the support they need to succeed in this new learning environment.

In conclusion, the digital age has revolutionized communication, offering unprecedented opportunities for connection and collaboration. However, it also presents unique challenges that require a new set of skills and strategies. By being mindful of our digital footprint, adapting to new technologies, communicating with empathy and clarity, and maintaining a healthy balance between online and offline interactions, we can harness the power of digital communication to build stronger relationships, foster greater understanding, and create a more connected world.

ᐅᐅᐅ

*Presentations are not just about information, but
about connection. Engage your audience, spark
their curiosity, and leave a lasting impression.*

ᐅᐅᐅ

THIRTEEN

LEADING WITH INFLUENCE: INSPIRING ACTION THROUGH COMMUNICATION

Leadership is not merely about holding a position of authority or wielding power. True leadership lies in the ability to influence and inspire others to action. It's about motivating individuals to achieve shared goals, fostering a sense of purpose, and creating a positive and productive environment. Communication is the cornerstone of influential leadership, the conduit through which leaders connect with their teams, articulate their vision, and rally support.

Leading with influence begins with effective communication. Leaders must be able to articulate their vision clearly and compellingly, painting a picture of the future that inspires and motivates others. This involves not only conveying the what but also the why – the purpose and meaning behind the goals and objectives.

When people understand the bigger picture and how their individual contributions fit into it, they are more likely to be engaged and committed to the cause.

Active listening is another crucial aspect of influential leadership. Leaders who genuinely listen to their team members create an environment of trust and respect. They show that they value the opinions and ideas of others, which in turn fosters a sense of ownership and empowerment. When people feel heard and understood, they are more likely to be invested in the success of the team.

Effective communication also involves adapting one's message to the audience. Leaders must be able to tailor their communication style to different individuals and groups, taking into account their diverse backgrounds, perspectives, and communication preferences. This might involve using different language, tone, or communication channels depending on the situation.

In addition to verbal communication, non-verbal cues play a significant role in influential leadership. Body language, facial expressions, and tone of voice can convey confidence, enthusiasm, and authenticity, or they can reveal doubt, disinterest, or insincerity. Leaders who are aware of their non-verbal communication can use it to reinforce their message and build trust with their team.

Building rapport and relationships is another essential aspect of leading with influence. Leaders who take the time to get to know their team members on a personal level create a stronger foundation for collaboration and trust. This involves showing genuine interest in their lives, asking questions, and actively listening to their responses. When people feel valued and appreciated, they are more likely to go above and beyond to achieve shared goals.

Effective feedback is also a critical component of influential leadership. Leaders must be able to provide both positive and constructive feedback in a way that is both supportive and motivating. This involves focusing on specific behaviors and outcomes, rather than personal attacks or generalizations. When feedback is delivered in a constructive and encouraging way, it can help individuals to identify areas for improvement and grow as professionals.

Leading with influence also involves empowering others. This means delegating tasks, providing resources and support, and trusting team members to do their best work. When leaders empower their teams, they foster a sense of ownership and accountability. This can lead to increased motivation, creativity, and innovation.

In times of change or uncertainty, influential leaders provide a sense of stability and direction. They communicate openly and transparently, acknowledge challenges, and offer solutions. They also inspire hope and optimism, even in the face of adversity. When leaders demonstrate resilience and determination, they can rally their teams and inspire them to persevere.

Influential leaders also understand the importance of celebrating successes. Recognizing and rewarding individual and team achievements can boost morale, strengthen team cohesion, and reinforce positive behaviors. It also sends a message that hard work and
dedication are valued and appreciated.

In conclusion, leading with influence is a multifaceted skill that requires effective communication, active listening, empathy, rapport building, empowerment, feedback, resilience, and celebration. Leaders who embody these qualities can inspire their teams to achieve great things, create a positive and productive work environment, and leave a lasting legacy.

By mastering the art of communication and building strong relationships, leaders can unlock the potential of their teams and achieve extraordinary results. Influential leadership is not about control or dominance; it's about inspiring others to become their best selves and work together towards a shared vision.

ᐅᐅᐅ

Networking is not about collecting contacts, but about cultivating relationships. Build bridges of trust, offer value, and create a supportive community.

ꔏꔏꔏ

FOURTEEN

Crafting Compelling Presentations: Engaging Your Audience from Start to Finish

The art of crafting a compelling presentation is a delicate balance of substance and style, information and inspiration. It's about captivating your audience from the moment you step on stage to the final slide, leaving a lasting impression and achieving your desired outcome. Whether you're pitching a business idea, sharing research findings, or simply trying to inform and entertain, the ability to deliver a compelling presentation is an invaluable skill that can open doors, influence decisions, and drive change.

A compelling presentation begins with a clear understanding of your audience. Who are they? What are their interests, needs, and expectations? What do you want them to know, feel, or do as a result of your presentation? By tailoring your message to your specific audience, you can ensure that your presentation resonates with them on a personal level and motivates them to action.

Once you understand your audience, the next step is to craft a clear and concise message. What is the main takeaway you want your audience to remember? What are the key points you want to convey? By distilling your message down to its essence, you can avoid overwhelming your audience with too much information and ensure that your message sticks.

A compelling presentation is not just about the content, it's also about the delivery. Your delivery style, body language, and voice can significantly impact how your message is received. A confident and enthusiastic delivery can engage and inspire your audience, while a monotonous or nervous delivery can quickly lose their attention.

The opening of your presentation is crucial for capturing your audience's attention and setting the stage for what's to come. A strong opening can be a powerful hook, an intriguing question, a surprising statistic, or a personal anecdote. The goal is to pique their curiosity, make them want to learn more, and keep them engaged throughout your presentation.

Once you have their attention, it's important to maintain it by delivering your content in a way that is both informative and engaging. This means using a variety of techniques to keep your audience interested, such as storytelling, humor, visuals, and interactive elements. It also means being mindful of your pacing and energy level, avoiding long, rambling monologues, and keeping your presentation focused and on track.

Visual aids can be a powerful tool for enhancing your presentation. Slides, images, videos, and other visuals can help to illustrate your points, reinforce your message, and keep your audience engaged. However, it's important to use visuals sparingly and strategically. Too many slides or overly complex visuals can distract from your message and overwhelm your audience.

The closing of your presentation is your final opportunity to leave a lasting impression on your audience. A strong closing can summarize your key points, reiterate your call to action, and leave your audience feeling inspired and motivated. It's also an opportunity to thank your audience for their time and attention.

In addition to these general tips, there are several specific techniques you can use to craft a compelling presentation. One effective technique is to use storytelling to connect with your audience on an emotional level. Stories can help to illustrate your points, make your message more memorable, and inspire your audience to action.

Another powerful technique is to use humor to lighten the mood and engage your audience. Humor can helpto break down barriers, build rapport, and make your presentation more enjoyable. However, it's important to use humor appropriately and avoid offensive or insensitive jokes.

Interactive elements can also be a great way to engage your audience. This could involve asking questions, soliciting feedback, or incorporating activities or games into your presentation. By involving your audience in the presentation, you can create a more dynamic and memorable experience.

Finally, it's important to practice your presentation beforehand. This will help you to become more familiar with your material, refine your delivery, and identify any areas that need improvement. Practicing in front of a friend, family member, or colleague can also provide valuable feedback and help you to feel more confident and prepared on the day of your presentation.

Crafting a compelling presentation is an art that requires a combination of creativity, preparation, and skill. By understanding your audience, crafting a clear and concise message, delivering your content with confidence and enthusiasm, and using effective techniques to engage your audience, you can create presentations that inform, inspire, and motivate.

ppp

Silence is not empty space, but a fertile ground for reflection. Embrace the stillness, listen to your inner voice, and find clarity within.

❥❥❥

FIFTEEN

Networking for Success: Building Relationships That Matter

Networking, often perceived as a transactional exchange of business cards, is a far more profound and enriching endeavor. It's about cultivating genuine connections, building relationships that matter, and creating a supportive community that can propel you towards your goals. Whether you're an aspiring entrepreneur, a seasoned professional, or simply someone looking to expand your social circle, networking can open doors, provide valuable insights, and offer a wealth of opportunities.

At its core, networking is about building relationships based on mutual respect, trust, and shared interests. It's not about collecting as many contacts as possible or attending every networking event in town. It's about focusing on quality over quantity, nurturing meaningful connections, and creating a network that truly supports your personal and professional growth.

Networking begins with a mindset shift. Instead of viewing networking as a necessary evil or a means to an end, approach it as an opportunity to connect with interesting people, learn new things, and expand your horizons. When you approach networking with genuine curiosity and a willingness to give back, you'll be surprised at the doors that open for you.

One of the most effective ways to network is to start with your existing network. Reach out to friends, family, colleagues, and former classmates. Let them know about your goals and interests, and ask for their advice and support. You might be surprised at how many people are willing to help you out or connect you with others who can.

Attend industry events, conferences, and workshops. These gatherings provide a great opportunity to meet like-minded individuals, learn about new trends and developments, and expand your knowledge and skills. Be sure to bring plenty of business cards and be prepared to introduce yourself and your work.

Join professional organizations and online communities. These groups can provide valuable resources, support, and networking opportunities. They can also help you stay up-to-date on industry news and trends.

Don't be afraid to reach out to people you admire. Whether it's a potential mentor, a thought leader in your field, or someone whose work you respect, reaching out can be a great way to expand your network and learn from the best. Be respectful of their time, be clear about your intentions, and offer something of value in return.

When networking, it's important to be genuine and authentic. People can sense when someone is being insincere or manipulative. Focus on building real relationships based on mutual respect and trust. This means being a good listener, showing genuine interest in others, and offering your support and expertise whenever possible.

Remember, networking is a two-way street. It's not just about what you can get from others, but also what you can give. Offer to help others with their projects, share your knowledge and expertise, and be a valuable resource for your network. The more you give, the more you'll receive in return.

Follow up with your new contacts. After meeting someone new, be sure to send a follow-up email or message to thank them for their time and express your interest in staying connected. This is a simple yet effective way to keep the conversation going and build a stronger relationship.

Networking is not a sprint, it's a marathon. It takes time and effort to build meaningful relationships. Be patient, persistent, and consistent in your efforts. The more you invest in your network, the more it will grow and flourish.

In today's interconnected world, networking is more important than ever. It can open doors to new opportunities, provide valuable insights, and offer a wealth of support and resources. By cultivating genuine connections and building relationships that matter, you can create a network that will propel you towards your goals and enrich your life in countless ways.

ppp

Humor is the sunshine of the soul. Share laughter, lighten the load, and brighten the world with your joyful spirit.

ᐁᐁᐁ

SIXTEEN

The Power of Silence: Creating Space for Reflection and Connection

In our modern world, characterized by constant noise and relentless stimulation, the power of silence often goes unnoticed and underappreciated. Yet, silence holds an immense capacity to enrich our lives, deepen our connections with others, and foster profound personal growth. It is in the quiet spaces that we find clarity, creativity, and a deeper understanding of ourselves and the world around us.

Silence is not merely the absence of sound; it is a presence in itself. It is a fertile ground for reflection and introspection, allowing us to slow down, tune into our inner world, and gain valuable insights. In the stillness of silence, we can hear the whispers of our own thoughts, feelings, and intuitions. We can process emotions, make sense of experiences, and connect with our deepest values and aspirations.

Silence also plays a crucial role in communication and connection. In conversations, pauses and moments of silence can create space for reflection, allowing both speaker and listener to fully absorb the meaning of the words spoken. Silence can also signal respect, empathy, and understanding. When we listen in silence, we give the other person the space to express themselves fully without interruption or judgment.

In relationships, silence can foster a deeper sense of intimacy and connection. Sharing quiet moments with a loved one can create a sense of closeness and understanding that words alone cannot convey. It allows us to be fully present with each other, to appreciate each other's company without the need for constant conversation.

In creative endeavors, silence is often the birthplace of inspiration. Artists, writers, and musicians often find that their most creative ideas emerge from moments of quiet contemplation. When we allow ourselves to be still and silent, we open our minds to new possibilities and allow our creativity to flow freely.

Silence can also be a powerful tool for healing and renewal. In times of stress, anxiety, or grief, silence can offer solace and comfort. It can help us to slow down, reconnect with our inner peace, and find the strength to move forward.

In our modern world, silence is becoming increasingly rare and valuable. We are constantly bombarded with information, notifications, and distractions. Our minds are rarely given the opportunity to rest and recharge. This constant stimulation can lead to stress, anxiety, burnout, and a sense of disconnection from ourselves and others.

By intentionally incorporating silence into our lives, we can counter these negative effects and reap the numerous benefits that silence has to offer. This might involve taking a few minutes each day to sit in silence, practicing mindfulness meditation, or simply turning off our electronic devices and enjoying the peace and quiet of nature.

Creating space for silence is not always easy. It requires a conscious effort to unplug from the constant noise and distractions of modern life. However, the rewards are well worth it. By embracing silence, we can tap into a deeper well of wisdom, creativity, and compassion. We can cultivate a more mindful and intentional way of living, and deepen our connections with ourselves, others, and the world around us.

In a world that is constantly urging us to do more, be more, and achieve more, the power of silence reminds us of the importance of simply being. It invites us to slow down, listen to our inner voice, and connect with the present moment. By embracing silence, we can discover a deeper sense of peace, joy, and fulfillment in our lives.

ᗸᗸᗸ

Cross-cultural communication is a dance of understanding. Embrace diversity, celebrate differences, and learn the steps of connection.

▷▷▷

SEVENTEEN

HUMOR AS A CONNECTOR: BRINGING JOY AND LIGHTNESS TO CONVERSATIONS

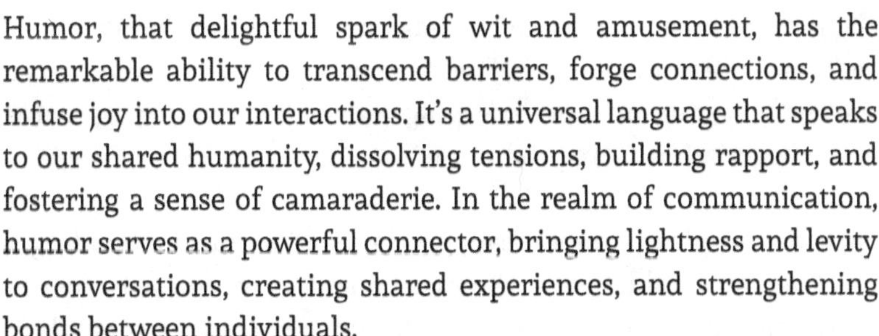

Humor, that delightful spark of wit and amusement, has the remarkable ability to transcend barriers, forge connections, and infuse joy into our interactions. It's a universal language that speaks to our shared humanity, dissolving tensions, building rapport, and fostering a sense of camaraderie. In the realm of communication, humor serves as a powerful connector, bringing lightness and levity to conversations, creating shared experiences, and strengthening bonds between individuals.

At its core, humor is about finding the funny in the mundane, the unexpected in the ordinary. It's about recognizing the absurdities of life and embracing them with a smile. When we laugh together, we share a moment of connection, a recognition of our shared human experience. Laughter releases endorphins, those feel-good chemicals in our brains, which not only uplift our mood but also reduce stress and anxiety.

Humor can break the ice and create instant rapport. A well-timed joke or a playful remark can disarm defensiveness, put people at ease, and create a more open and receptive atmosphere. It can help to defuse tension, bridge differences, and build bridges of understanding. When we share a laugh with someone, we create a sense of camaraderie and shared experience, laying the foundation for a deeper connection.

In conversations, humor can serve as a social lubricant, smoothing over awkward moments, diffusing disagreements, and fostering a sense of lightheartedness. A witty remark or a self-deprecating joke can break down barriers, making us more approachable and relatable. It can also signal that we don't take ourselves too seriously, inviting others to let their guard down and engage in a more relaxed and authentic way.

Humor can also be a powerful tool for persuasion and influence. When we use humor effectively, we can disarm our audience, make them more receptive to our message, and increase the likelihood that they will remember what we have to say. A touch of humor can make a presentation more engaging, a sales pitch more persuasive, and a negotiation more productive.

In the workplace, humor can play a crucial role in building a positive and productive work environment. A well-timed joke can boost morale, reduce stress, and foster a sense of camaraderie among team members. It can also help to break down hierarchical barriers, creating a more relaxed and collaborative atmosphere.

In our personal lives, humor can strengthen our relationships with friends and family. Sharing a laugh with a loved one can create a sense of intimacy and connection that goes beyond words. It can also help us to navigate difficult conversations, diffuse conflict, and build resilience in the face of adversity.

While humor can be a powerful tool for connection, it's important to use it with care and sensitivity. Humor that is offensive, discriminatory, or hurtful can damage relationships and create a hostile environment. It's important to be mindful of our audience and to avoid jokes or remarks that might be perceived as insensitive or inappropriate.

The best kind of humor is often self-deprecating, playful, and inclusive. It's about finding the funny in our own foibles and imperfections, and inviting others to laugh along with us. It's about creating a shared experience of joy and amusement, where everyone feels included and appreciated.

In a world that is often filled with stress, anxiety, and conflict, humor can be a powerful antidote. It can bring joy and lightness to our interactions, build bridges of understanding, and foster a sense of connection and community. By embracing the power of humor, we can create a more positive and fulfilling life for ourselves and those around us.

ᐯᐯᐯ

Communication is a lifelong journey of learning and growth. Embrace the challenges, seek new perspectives, and evolve into a master communicator.

❧❧❧

EIGHTEEN

Cross-Cultural Communication: Bridging Differences with Understanding

In an increasingly interconnected world, cross-cultural communication has become an essential skill. As we interact with people from diverse backgrounds, we need to be able to bridge cultural divides and communicate effectively with those who may have different customs, values, and perspectives. This ability to navigate cultural differences with understanding is not only crucial for personal relationships but also for successful business interactions, diplomacy, and global cooperation.

At its core, cross-cultural communication is about recognizing and respecting the diversity of human experience. It involves understanding that people from different cultures may have different ways of communicating, different values and beliefs, and different ways of seeing the world. This awareness allows us to approach interactions with an open mind and a willingness to learn from others.

One of the key challenges of cross-cultural communication is the potential for misunderstanding. Language barriers, cultural norms, and differing communication styles can all contribute to misinterpretations and miscommunications. To avoid these pitfalls, it's important to be mindful of our own cultural biases and assumptions, and to be willing to adapt our communication style to the cultural context.

Language is a powerful tool for communication, but it can also be a source of misunderstanding. Words and phrases can have different meanings in different cultures, and even subtle differences in pronunciation or intonation can lead to misinterpretations. To overcome language barriers, it's important to speak clearly and simply, avoid using slang or jargon, and be patient with those who may not be fluent in our language.

Non-verbal communication, such as body language, facial expressions, and gestures, can also vary significantly across cultures. What might be considered polite or respectful in one culture might be seen as rude or offensive in another. To avoid misunderstandings, it's important to be aware of the non-verbal cues that are common in the culture you are interacting with and to adapt your own behavior accordingly.

Cultural norms and values can also significantly impact communication. Different cultures may have different expectations regarding formality, directness, and the expression of emotions. For example, in some cultures, it's considered rude to be too direct or confrontational, while in others, directness is valued as a sign of honesty and sincerity. Understanding these cultural norms can help us to communicate in a way that is respectful and appropriate.

Building trust is essential for effective cross-cultural communication. When we trust someone, we are more likely to be open to their perspective, even if it differs from our own. To build trust, it's important to be honest, reliable, and respectful. We should also be willing to listen to others' perspectives and to acknowledge their feelings and concerns.

Another important aspect of cross-cultural communication is the ability to adapt to different communication styles. Some cultures may prefer a more indirect or high-context communication style, where meaning is conveyed through subtle cues and unspoken understandings. Other cultures may prefer a more direct or low-context communication style, where meaning is explicitly stated through words. By being aware of these different styles, we can adapt our communication to the preferences of the person we are interacting with.

In the workplace, cross-cultural communication is essential for building diverse and inclusive teams. When employees from different backgrounds feel valued and respected, they are more likely to be engaged and productive. By fostering a culture of cross-cultural understanding, organizations can tap into a wider range of perspectives and ideas, leading to greater innovation and success.

In our personal lives, cross-cultural communication can enrich our relationships and broaden our horizons. By interacting with people from different cultures, we can learn about new customs, traditions, and ways of life. We can also challenge our own assumptions and biases, leading to greater self-awareness and personal growth.

Cross-cultural communication is not always easy, but it is a skill that can be learned and developed through practice and a willingness to learn from others. By embracing diversity, seeking to understand different perspectives, and adapting our communication style to the cultural context, we can build bridges of understanding and create a more harmonious and interconnected world.

ᐅᐅᐅ

Your legacy is not what you leave behind, but what you create within others. Inspire, empower, and leave a trail of positive impact.

❥❥❥

NINETEEN

THE LIFETIME JOURNEY OF COMMUNICATION: CONTINUOUS LEARNING AND GROWTH

Communication is not a destination, but a lifelong journey. It is a dynamic and ever-evolving process that requires constant learning, adaptation, and growth. From the moment we utter our first words as infants to the wisdom we share in our later years, communication shapes our relationships, careers, and personal development.

Embracing this journey with an open mind and a willingness to learn can lead to profound personal and interpersonal transformations.

In the early stages of life, communication is primarily about expressing basic needs and emotions. As infants, we cry to signal hunger, discomfort, or a desire for attention. As we grow, we learn to use words to express our thoughts and feelings, to ask questions, and to interact with others.

This early development of communication skills lays the foundation for our future interactions and relationships.

As we enter childhood and adolescence, communication becomes increasingly complex. We learn to navigate social situations, express our opinions, and negotiate with others. We also begin to develop our own unique communication style, influenced by our family, culture, and personal experiences.

This is a time of experimentation and exploration, as we try out different ways of communicating and discover what works best for us.

During adulthood, communication takes on new dimensions as we enter the workforce, build relationships, and raise families. We learn to communicate effectively in professional settings, to negotiate contracts, to give presentations, and to lead teams.

We also learn to communicate with our partners, children, and loved ones in a way that fosters intimacy, trust, and understanding.

As we age, communication continues to evolve. We may face new challenges, such as hearing loss or cognitive decline, that require us to adapt our communication strategies. We may also find that our communication needs and preferences change as we enter different stages of life.

Throughout our lives, we are constantly learning new ways to communicate. We learn from our successes and our failures, from our interactions with others, and from the feedback we receive. We also learn from books, articles, workshops, and other educational resources.

One of the most important aspects of the communication journey is the willingness to learn and grow. This means being open to feedback, trying new approaches, and stepping outside of our comfort zone. It also means being patient with ourselves and others, recognizing that communication is a skill that takes time and practice to master.

As we continue to learn and grow, our communication skills can become increasingly sophisticated. We can learn to communicate with greater clarity, empathy, and effectiveness. We can also develop the ability to adapt our communication style to different situations and audiences.

Effective communication is not just about transmitting information; it's about building relationships, fostering understanding, and creating positive change. When we communicate effectively, we can resolve conflicts, build trust, inspire others, and achieve our goals.

In the workplace, effective communication is essential for success. Employees who can communicate clearly and persuasively are more likely to be promoted and to have their ideas heard. They are also more likely to build strong relationships with their colleagues and clients.

In our personal lives, effective communication is the foundation of healthy relationships. When we communicate openly and honestly with our loved ones, we build trust, intimacy, and connection. We also create a safe space for sharing our thoughts, feelings, and experiences.

The journey of communication is a lifelong adventure. It is a journey filled with challenges, opportunities, and rewards.

By embracing this journey with an open mind and a willingness to learn, we can develop the skills we need to connect with others on a deeper level, achieve our goals, and make a positive impact on the world.

ppp

*Connection is the heart of human existence.
Embrace it, nurture it, and let it illuminate your
path to a more fulfilling life.*

❥❥❥

TWENTY

CREATING A LEGACY OF CONNECTION: MAKING A POSITIVE IMPACT THROUGH YOUR WORDS AND ACTIONS

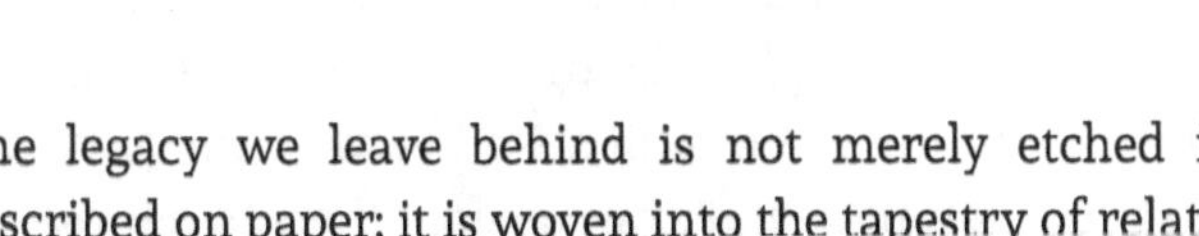

The legacy we leave behind is not merely etched in stone or inscribed on paper; it is woven into the tapestry of relationships we cultivate and the impact we have on the lives of others. Creating a legacy of connection involves recognizing the profound power of our words and actions to shape the world around us. It is about using our communication skills to uplift, inspire, and empower others, leaving a positive imprint that extends far beyond our own lifetimes.

At its core, a legacy of connection is built upon the foundation of genuine relationships. It is about fostering meaningful connections with the people we encounter, both personally and professionally. This involves investing time and energy in building trust, understanding, and mutual respect. It means being present for others, listening to their stories, and offering support and encouragement.

Our words have the power to build bridges or create barriers. When we choose to speak with kindness, compassion, and empathy, we create a space for open dialogue and collaboration. We foster a sense of belonging and connection, where everyone feels heard and valued. On the other hand, words that are harsh, judgmental, or divisive can wound and alienate others, leaving lasting scars and creating rifts in relationships.

Actions speak louder than words, and the actions we take can have a profound impact on the world around us. Whether it's volunteering our time to help those in need, advocating for social justice, or simply offering a helping hand to a friend, our actions can create a ripple effect of positivity that extends far beyond our immediate circle.

Creating a legacy of connection involves aligning our words and actions with our values and beliefs. It means living a life that is congruent with our principles, being true to ourselves, and inspiring others to do the same. When we live with integrity and authenticity, we create a powerful example for others to follow.

One of the most powerful ways to create a legacy of connection is through mentorship and leadership. By sharing our knowledge, experience, and wisdom with others, we can empower them to achieve their goals and make a positive impact on the world. Whether it's mentoring a young professional, coaching a sports team, or simply offering guidance to a friend, our willingness to invest in others can have a lasting impact on their lives.

Another way to create a legacy of connection is through storytelling. Stories have the power to connect us to one another on a deep emotional level. They can inspire, motivate, and challenge us to think differently about the world. By sharing our own stories, we can inspire others to share theirs, creating a tapestry of shared experiences and interconnectedness.

Building a legacy of connection also involves leaving a positive mark on our communities and the world at large. This might involve volunteering our time and talents to organizations that support causes we believe in, advocating for social justice, or simply being a good neighbor and friend. By contributing to the well-being of our communities, we create a legacy that extends far beyond our own lifetimes.

In the digital age, creating a legacy of connection also involves using our online platforms to promote positive messages and connect with others in meaningful ways. We can use social media to share inspiring stories, support causes we care about, and connect with people from all walks of life. By using our online presence for good, we can create a ripple effect of positivity that extends far beyond our own screens.

Creating a legacy of connection is not about achieving fame or fortune. It's about living a life of purpose, meaning, and impact. It's about using our words and actions to make the world a better place, one interaction at a time. Whether it's through our work, our relationships, or our community involvement, we can all leave a legacy that will be remembered and cherished long after we are gone.

In the end, the legacy we leave behind is not measured by the size of our bank accounts or the number of awards we receive. It is measured by the depth of our relationships, the impact we have on others, and the positive change we create in the world. By choosing to live a life of connection, compassion, and service, we can create a legacy that will inspire generations to come.

ᐅᐅᐅ

Stories are the threads that weave the tapestry of humanity. Share your stories, listen to others', and create a vibrant tapestry of connection.

❦❦❦

TWENTY-ONE
SUMMARY

Mastering communication is an art form that extends far beyond mere words. It's a symphony of presence, empathy, understanding, and connection. Throughout this exploration, we have delved into the intricate layers of communication, uncovering the power of presence, the importance of empathy, and the art of decoding non-verbal cues. We have explored the significance of crafting messages with clarity and compassion, asking powerful questions, and finding our authentic voice. We have learned how to navigate conflict with grace, weave captivating narratives, build rapport, and give and receive feedback as a gift. We have delved into the art of apology, the nuances of communication in the digital age, and the power of leading with influence. We have also explored the art of storytelling, networking for success, the power of silence, the role of humor as a connector, and the importance of cross-cultural understanding. Finally, we have embarked on the lifelong journey of communication, recognizing that it is a continuous process of learning and growth, culminating in the creation of a legacy of connection through our words and actions.

Presence, the act of being fully present with another person, is the foundation of effective communication. It involves active listening, paying attention to non-verbal cues, and creating a space where the other person feels heard and valued. Empathy, the ability to understand and share the feelings of others, is another essential component of communication. It allows us to connect with others on a deeper level, build trust, and resolve conflicts.

Non-verbal communication, often referred to as the silent language of connection, plays a significant role in our interactions. Facial expressions, body language, tone of voice, and other non-verbal cues can convey a wealth of information about our thoughts and feelings. By learning to decode these cues, we can gain a deeper understanding of others and communicate more effectively.

Words have the power to build bridges or create barriers. Crafting messages with clarity and compassion involves choosing our words carefully, being mindful of our tone, and seeking to understand the perspective of others. Asking powerful questions can ignite curiosity, deepen conversations, and foster meaningful connections. By asking open-ended questions, we invite others to share their thoughts and feelings, leading to greater understanding and collaboration.

Finding our authentic voice is a journey of self-discovery and self-expression. It involves embracing our unique perspective, speaking our truth with confidence, and aligning our words with our values and beliefs. When we communicate authentically, we build trust, inspire others, and create a lasting impact.

Conflict is an inevitable part of human interaction, but it doesn't have to be destructive. By navigating conflict with grace, we can transform challenges into opportunities for growth and understanding. This involves effective communication, empathy, forgiveness, and a willingness to find solutions that work for everyone involved.

Storytelling is a powerful tool for communication. By weaving narratives that captivate and inspire, we can connect with others on a deeper level, convey complex ideas, and motivate action. Building rapport involves creating instant connections with others through active listening, mirroring, finding common ground, asking open-ended questions, sharing personal stories, and using humor.

In the digital age, communication has taken on new dimensions. While technology has made it easier to connect with people across the globe, it has also created new challenges. To communicate effectively in the digital landscape, we need to be mindful of our digital footprint, adapt to new technologies, and communicate with empathy and clarity.

Leading with influence involves inspiring action through communication. By articulating a clear vision, actively listening to others, building rapport, providing feedback, empowering others, and celebrating successes, leaders can motivate their teams to achieve extraordinary results.

Crafting compelling presentations involves engaging your audience from start to finish. This involves understanding your audience, crafting a clear and concise message, delivering your content with confidence and enthusiasm, and using visuals and interactive elements to enhance your presentation.

Networking for success involves building relationships that matter. This involves focusing on quality over quantity, nurturing meaningful connections, and creating a network that truly supports your personal and professional growth. By being genuine, offering value, and following up with your contacts, you can build a network that will open doors to new opportunities and enrich your life in countless ways.

The power of silence lies in its ability to create space for reflection and connection. In the stillness of silence, we can gain valuable insights, process emotions, and connect with our deepest values and aspirations. By intentionally incorporating silence into our lives, we can reduce stress, improve our focus, and deepen our relationships with ourselves and others.

Humor is a universal language that can connect people across cultures and backgrounds. By bringing joy and lightness to conversations, humor can break down barriers, diffuse tension, and foster a sense of camaraderie. It can also make our communication more engaging, persuasive, and memorable.

Cross-cultural communication is essential in our increasingly interconnected world. By recognizing and respecting cultural differences, we can bridge divides, build trust, and communicate effectively with people from all walks of life.

The journey of communication is a lifelong endeavor. By embracing this journey with an open mind and a willingness to learn, we can continuously improve our communication skills, deepen our connections with others, and create a legacy of connection that will last for generations to come.

ᗜᗜᗜ

Citation And References

This book represents the culmination of extensive research and meticulous analysis, incorporating a diverse range of sources, including numerous books, scholarly studies, and personal experiences. Additionally, I have scoured various websites to gather relevant information and data essential for the compilation of this work. I have taken every precaution to ensure the accuracy of the information presented and have diligently cited all sources to acknowledge their contributions.

Despite these efforts, the possibility of inadvertent errors remains. I deeply value the insights of my readers and appreciate any feedback that can help identify and rectify such inaccuracies. I encourage you to bring any discrepancies to my attention.

Your feedback is not only welcome but crucial, as it will aid in correcting current editions and enhancing the content of future ones. I am committed to maintaining the highest standards of accuracy and reliability in my work and thank you for your support and understanding.

Additionally, I firmly uphold the principle of freedom of speech and expression as guaranteed under Article 19(1)(a) of the Constitution of India, and I respect the diverse viewpoints and expressions of all readers.

ᐳᐳᐳ

Other Books Of The Author

1. Empowering Minds: A Journey into Women's Self-Discovery and Power
2. The Dynamics of Motivation: Catalyzing Thought into Action
3. Meditation and Mental Well Being: The Path to Inner Peace and Clarity
4. The Psychology of Child Education: Nurturing Future Generations
5. Ethical Enlightenment: A Modern Guide to Living with Integrity
6. Voices of Empowerment: Stories of Women Rising Against Odds
7. Social Psychology in Everyday Life: Understanding Human Connections
8. The Essence of Motivational Speaking: Inspiring Change in Others
9. Balancing Acts: Women, Work, and the Will to Lead
10. Guiding with Grace: Raising Children with Compassion and Awareness
11. The Power of Positive Aging: Embracing Life After Fifty
12. Building Resilient Communities: Social Work in Action
13. The Ethical Educator: Principles for Teaching and Learning
14. From Insight to Impact: Social Psychology for a Better World
15. The Ethics of Empathy: A Guide to Ethical Living
16. The Science of Empowering the Self: Navigating Life's Challenges with Psychological Wisdom
17. The Mindful Conscious Leader: Meditation Techniques for Modern Management
18. Pioneering Spirit: Women's Pathways to Leadership and Empowerment
19. Feeling to Healing: The Role of Emotional Intelligence in Child Development
20. Transformative Talks and Words of Inspiration: Insights into Motivational Oratory

21. Green Ethics: A Path to Sustainable Living
22. Spiritual Integrity: Navigating Life with Moral Compassion
23. Clean Living, Clean Society: The Ethics of Cleanliness
24. Patriotic Spirits: Building a Nation on Positive Attitudes
25. Innovative Integrity & Vibrant Visions: The Ethical and Entrepreneurial Spirit of Gujarat
26. Youthful Visions, Endless Possibilities: Inspiring Ethics and Motivation in Children
27. Living Your Legacy: How to Motivate Others by Living Your Values
28. Secret of Healing Conversations: Ethical Practices in Counselling and Therapy
29. Creative Kindness: Crafting a Life of Compassion and Creativity
30. The Power of Appreciation: How Gratitude Can Transform Your Relationships
31. Bhagavad-Gita: Messages
32. Science of Art: The New Frontier of Fashion Modernism
33. Vivekananda's Virtues: A Blueprint for Modern Living
34. Empower Her: Navigating the Path to Women's Entrepreneurship
35. The Boundless Classroom: Innovations in Global Education
36. The Language of Leadership: Communicating with Authenticity and Impact
37. The Warrior's Mantra: Deciphering the Hanuman Chalisa
38. Echoes of Empathy: Transformative Stories of Social Service
39. Artful Living: Cultivating Creativity in Your Daily Routine
40. Finding Your Why: Discovering Your Passions and Charting Your Course
41. The Role of Social Media in Shaping Self-Esteem and Interpersonal Relationships among Adolescents
42. Karma's Tapestry: Weaving a Life of Selfless Service
43. Altruistic Alchemy: Transforming Lives Through Giving
44. The Blueprint of Pro-Activeness and Productivity: Crafting Habits for Success
45. The Simplicity with Grounded Wisdom: Embracing Authenticity

in a Complex World

46. Secret of Solopreneur's Odyssey: Navigating the Path to Self-Employment
47. Exploring Tapestry of Peace: Global Perspectives on Harmony
48. The Art and Actions of Connection: Mastering Communication for Impact
49. She Governs and at the Helm: Strategies for Political Empowerment
50. Rising Above and Rising with Grace: A Woman's Roadmap to Career Mastery
51. The Effect of Networking & Connectedness: Building Strategic Alliances for Women
52. Beyond his Barriers: Women Thriving in Male-Dominated Fields
53. Secret of Inner Compass: Navigating Life with Intuition
54. Creative & Pro-Active Muses: A Celebration of Women in the Arts
55. Unburdened: The Art of Releasing the Past
56. Amplified Voices: Speeches of Women that Astonished the World
57. Secret of Manifesting Dreams: A Woman's Guide to Intentional Living
58. Ethics and Value Based Education: Reimagining Japan's School System
59. The Moral Compass Curriculum: A Holistic Approach
60. Tech with Heart: Integrating Ethics into Digital Learning
61. Honoring Virtue: Recognizing Ethical Excellence in Education
62. Raising Good Humans: A Guide to Character Development
63. The Spark Within: Nurturing Creativity in Children
64. The Teenager Whisperer: Navigating Adolescence with Grace
65. Igniting a Passion for Learning: Inspiring Lifelong Curiosity
66. The Habit Lab: Cultivating Positive Behaviors in Children
67. Seeds of Empathy: Fostering Compassion in Young Hearts
68. The Reading Revolution: Inspiring a Love of Books in Children
69. The Learning Brain: Unlocking the Secrets of Student Success
70. Teaching for All: Differentiated Instruction Strategies
71. The Time Alchemist: Mastering Time Management for Peak Performance

72. The Resilience Factor: Transforming Setbacks into Stepping Stones
73. The Healing Touch of Nature: An Introduction to Naturopathy
74. Echoes of the Past: Healing Through Past Life Regression
75. The Spiritual Healer's Handbook: Exploring Energy Medicine
76. Crystal Clarity: Unveiling the Power of Gemstones
77. The Dream Weaver's Guide: Decoding the Language of Dreams
78. Emotional Alchemy: Transforming Pain into Power
79. Sonic Serenity: Harnessing Sound for Stress Relief
80. The Entrepreneur's Playbook: Launching Your Business with Confidence
81. Productivity Unleashed: Time Management Strategies for Entrepreneurs
82. The Problem Solver's Toolkit: Creative Solutions for Business Challenges
83. The Future is Now: Emerging Trends in Business
84. The Curious Explorer: A Child's Guide to Scientific Discovery
85. Digital Pioneers: Empowering Kids in the Tech World
86. The Young Philosopher's Guide: Exploring Life's Big Questions
87. Finding Your Voice: Communication Skills for Confident Kids
88. Nature's Playground: A Child's Guide to Outdoor Adventure
89. Growing a Greener Tomorrow: A Guide to Tree Planting & Conservation
90. Driving with Purpose: Ethical Choices on the Road
91. The Healing Touch: Cultivating Compassion in Healthcare
92. Navigating the Digital Landscape: Ethics in the Age of Social Media
93. The Ethical Closet: A Guide to Sustainable Fashion
94. The Mindful Voyager: Sustainable Travel Practices
95. The Feminine Divine: Honoring the Goddesses of India
96. Sacred Sounds: Chanting Your Way to Inner Peace
97. The Yoga Path: Uniting with the Divine Within
98. Rites of Passage: Creating Meaningful Ceremonies
99. The Chakra System: A Map of Inner Transformation
100. Spiritual Sangha: Finding Community through Satsang and

Bhajan

101. Pilgrimage of the Soul: Spiritual Journeys in India

❧❧❧

Contact

Dr. Minakshi Bansal
Social Activist
Ahmedabad, Gujarat, Bharat
minakshiindiag20@yahoo.com

❧❧❧

|| LOKAHA SAMASTHAHA SUKHINO BHAVANTU ||